TAO TÊ CHING

M
A
N
D
A
L
A

This translation of the Tao Tê Ching by Ch'u
Ta-Kao, the first by a modern Chinese scholar,
powerfully conveys the beauty and vigour of
the original. It is illustrated with sympathetic
and original woodcuts by Willow Winston.
General comments on chapters and footnotes
appear at the end of the book.

TAO TÊ CHING

TAO TÊ CHING

Translated from the Chinese by

CH'U TA-KAO

Illustrated
by
Willow Winston

MANDALA

UNWIN PAPERBACKS

London   Boston   Sydney   Wellington

First published by George Allen & Unwin 1959
Reprinted 1970
First published in paperback 1972
First published in Unwin Paperbacks 1976
Illustrated edition first published 1982
This Mandala edition 1985
Reprinted 1986
Reissued 1989

UNWIN HYMAN LIMITED
15–17 Broadwick Street, London W1V 1FP

Allen & Unwin Australia Pty Ltd,.
8 Napier Street, North Sydney, NSW 2060, Australia

Allen & Unwin New Zealand Pty Ltd with the Port Nicholson Press
Compusales Building, 75 Ghuznee Street, Wellington, New Zealand

Unwin Hyman Inc
8 Winchester Place, Winchester MA 01890, USA

Parts of this reset edition
© George Allen & Unwin (Publishers) Ltd 1970, 1982, 1985

Illustrations © Willow Winston 1982, 1985

ISBN 0 04 299012 2

A CIP Catalogue record is available from the British Library

Printed and bound in Great Britain
by Cox & Wyman Ltd, Reading

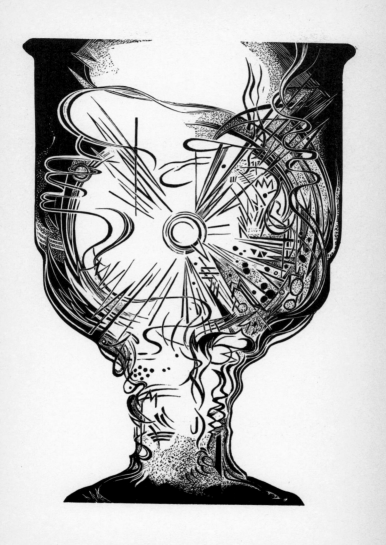

Foreword

BY DR LIONEL GILES

Formerly Keeper of the Oriental Manuscripts
at the British museum

No book in the world, perhaps, with the exception of
the Bible, has been translated so often as the *Tao Tê
Ching*. What is the secret of its perennial fascination?
This little treatise of about 5,000 characters may or
may not have been the work of a philosopher
contemporary with Confucius, known to us as Lao
Tzu. Modern critics incline to give it a much later
date, and in its present form it certainly suggests the
third rather than the sixth century B.C. But it is
strangely unlike any other production of the Chou
era that has come down to us. The structure of the
work is in the highest degree incoherent: it is a
collection of aphorisms jumbled together with little
or no attempt at an orderly arrangement, and even
the division into chapters (which is probably a later
addition) helps hardly at all. The whole gist of the
book is the glorification of simplicity, yet it contains
passage after passage of the most baffling obscurity,
and the numerous translations often differ so widely
that they hardly seem to represent one and the same
text. Perhaps it is this very absence of finality, this
unlimited variety of interpretation, that has proved
so alluring. At any rate, though mirrored in the facets
of many minds, the sayings of Lao Tzu remain as
enigmatical as ever.

The wording of the original is extraordinarily

vigorous and terse: never, surely, has so much thought been compressed into so small a space. Throughout the universe there are scattered a certain number of stars belonging to a class known as 'white dwarfs'. They are usually very small, yet the atoms of which they consist are crushed together so closely that their weight is enormous in relation to their size, and this entails the radiation of so much energy that the surface is kept at a temperature vastly hotter than that of the sun. The *Tao Tê Ching* may fitly be called a 'white dwarf' of philosophical literature, so weighty is it, so compact, and so suggestive of a mind radiating thought at a white heat.

Of most previous translators it may be said that 'despite their sagacity they have gone far astray'. Some have tried in vain to emulate the conciseness of the Chinese, others have usurped the functions of the commentator, and become flabby and diffuse. The present translation avoids these mistakes. Like the Great Way itself, it is plain and smooth, and does not diverge into by-paths. It gives us Lao Tzu's words so far as possible unchanged, and lets us judge of their inner meaning for ourselves. A further source of interest is the fact that the translator is of the same race as the author of the work; it is, I believe, the first time that a rendering of the *Tao Tê Ching* by a native of China has been published in this country.

LIONEL GILES

Translator's Preface

There are several factors which make it an extremely difficult task to translate Lao Tzu's *Tao Tê Ching*. First, the book is one of the few ancient Chinese writings that survive today. The mere space of time makes one apprehend the difficulty of approaching it. Secondly, though it is recorded in history that Confucius had seen Lao Tzu, he did not include the *Tao Tê Ching* in the Classics he edited; and because its principles disagree with those of the Confucian school, later editors, most of whom were Confucians, would not raise it to the order of Classics, which alone had the widest circulation among Chinese books. Thirdly, neither the language, which is to some extent different from and more difficult than that in which other old works were written, nor the philosophy were familiar to those scholars who were only acquainted with the Classics. Fourthly, before paper was invented in China, books were usually written on bamboo-tablets and fastened with strings or strips of leather. While being handed down from generation to generation the tablets were from time to time displaced, and the disarrangement caused distortions to the text. Fifthly, the Chinese system of writing had undergone a number of changes between the earliest times and the third century B.C.; the text of the *Tao Tê Ching* was written in an older and more difficult calligraphic style, and many of the characters bore a different meaning from that of their later forms. In transcribing them editors must have made mistakes or substituted some of the old

11

characters for new ones which do not mean the same thing. Sixthly, until very recently no punctuation was used in Chinese writing, and such ambiguities as abound in classical syntax may easily result in different readings. That is why for hundreds of years the editors and commentators of the *Tao Tê Ching* have never completely agreed with one another as to the text and meaning of this mysterious work.

These and a number of other difficulties and controversies have led recent scholars to dispute even the identity of the author, and to doubt the authenticity of the work. This, however, concerns us very little. Suffice it to say that it was probably written during or some time after Confucius' day by somebody called Lao Tzu. What matters most to us is the book itself, the philosophy of which does represent the mind of a certain period in the past and ever since has influenced the life and thought of the Chinese people.

Of the original text of this book, unfortunately, little is known. It is true that the edition of Wang Pi is the earliest of which we can avail ourselves, but it is not safe to assert that his is perfectly genuine and sound. On the contrary, the text of Wang's edition is marred by absolutely indefensible corruptions. For instance, a number of characters that appear in his text had not come into use in olden times; in some chapters the words (characters) commented upon are not the same as the corresponding ones in the text; in other cases the passages mentioned in the commentary do not exist in the text. Similar and sometimes more serious corruptions are also found in the other texts of later date. It is hardly possible to read or translate the book from any one text only. In fact, few editors or translators have ever been able to resist the temptation of 'touching up' the text to accord with the result of their own researches. This, however, is harmless and encourageable. For only in this way we can hope to get at the original. (For the same reason editors of Shakespeare, since the First Folio, continue to bring out new editions – Rowe, Malone, the New Shakespeare, and so on.)

During the last two centuries scholars of Lao Tzu have furnished a considerable amount of valuable material for the emendation of the *Tao Tê Ching* text. This material has recently been collected for the first time by a contemporary scholar, Mr Ch'ên Chu, into one book (published 1930, Shanghai), which accumulates all the reliable researches and comments of former and present-day scholars, such as Wang Pi, Fu Yi, Pi Yüan, Wang Nien-sun, Ma Hsü-lun, Lo Chênyu, Hu Shih, etc., in addition to his own erudition. It is an attempt to restore the original text. For in this edition the corruptions of former texts have been recorrected, and in a few cases the passages of one chapter transferred to another to make them coherent, on the grounds that they had been misread or become disarranged, as described above. The present translation is based mainly on Mr Che'ên's reading but in a few places where opinions differ I have preferred the readings of other scholars. I believe that this new edition throws more light on the *Tao Tê Ching*, and renders its contents more consistent and intelligible than any other I know.

Modern scholars agree that in the original book there were neither division of chapters nor sub-titles preceding them. These were all supplied by successive editors. In the present translation, however, for the convenience of reference I give the numbers of chapters as they were in former editions.

My special thanks are due to Mr and Mrs Christmas Humphreys, whose encouragement alone has effectuated my translation, and also to Prof. A. C. Moule and Mr Alan W. Watts, who have kindly gone through the MS. and made many valuable suggestions. I am also grateful to Mr Ch'ên Chu and the Commercial Press, Shanghai, for their permission to use the text.

CH'U TA-KAO

Cambridge

TAO TÊ CHING

CHAPTER 1

The Tao that can be expressed is not the eternal Tao;
The name that can be defined is not the unchanging
name.[1]
Non-existence[2] is called the antecedent of heaven
and earth;
Existence is the mother of all things.
From eternal non-existence, therefore, we serenely
observe the mysterious beginning of the Universe;
From eternal existence we clearly see the apparent
distinctions.
These two are the same in source and become
different when manifested.
This sameness is called profundity.[3] Infinite profundity is the gate whence comes the beginning of all
parts of the Universe.

CHAPTER 2

When all in the world understand beauty to be
   beautiful, then ugliness exists.
When all understand goodness to be good, then evil
   exists.
Thus existence suggests non-existence;
Easy gives rise to difficult;
Short is derived from long by comparison;
Low is distinguished from high by position;
Resonance harmonizes sound;
After follows before.
Therefore, the Sage carries on his business without
   action, and gives his teaching without words.[1]

CHAPTER 3

Not exalting the worthy keeps the people from emulation. Not valuing rare things keeps them from theft. Not showing what is desirable keeps their hearts from confusion. Therefore the Sage rules
By emptying their hearts,
Filling their stomachs,
Weakening their ambitions
And strengthening their bones.
He always keeps them from knowing what is evil and desiring what is good; thus he gives the crafty ones no chance to act. He governs by non-action; consequently there is nothing un-governed.

CHAPTER 4

Tao, when put in use for its hollowness, is not likely
    to be filled.
In its profundity it seems to be the origin of all things.
In its depth it seems ever to remain.
I do not know whose offspring it is;
But it looks like the predecessor of Nature.

CHAPTER 5

Heaven and earth do not own their benevolence;
To them all things are straw-dogs.[1]
The Sage does not own his benevolence;
To him the people are straw-dogs.

The space between heaven and earth is like a
  (blacksmith's) bellows.
Hollow as it seems, nothing is lacking.
If it is moved, more will it bring forth.[2]

He who talks more is sooner exhausted.
It is better to keep what is within himself.[3]

CHAPTER 6

'The Valley and the Spirit never die.'
They form what is called the Mystic Mother,
From whose gate comes the origin of heaven and
earth.
This (the origin) seems ever to endure.
In use it can never be exhausted.

CHAPTER 7

Heaven is lasting and earth enduring.
The reason why they are lasting and enduring is that
    they do not live for themselves;
Therefore they live long.
In the same way the Sage keeps himself behind and
    he is in the front;
He forgets himself and he is preserved.
Is it not because he is not self-interested
That his self-interest is established?

CHAPTER 8

The highest goodness is like water. Water is beneficent to all things but does not contend. It stays in places which others despise. Therefore it is near Tao.

In dwelling, think it a good place to live;
In feeling, make the heart deep;
In friendship, keep on good terms with men;
In words, have confidence;
In ruling, abide by good order;
In business, take things easy;
In motion, make use of the opportunity.
Since there is no contention, there is no blame.

CHAPTER 9

Holding and keeping a thing to the very full – it is
    better to leave it alone;
Handling and sharpening a blade – it cannot be long
    sustained;
When gold and jade fill the hall, no one can protect
    them;
Wealth and honour with pride bring with them
    destruction;
To have accomplished merit and acquired fame, then
    to retire –
This is the Tao of heaven.

CHAPTER 10

Can you keep the soul always concentrated from
  straying?
Can you regulate the breath and become soft and
  pliant like an infant?
Can you clear and get rid of the unforeseen and be
  free from fault?
Can you love the people and govern the state by non-
  action?
Can you open and shut the gates of nature like a
  female?
Can you become enlightened and penetrate everywhere without knowledge?

CHAPTER 11

Thirty spokes unite in one nave,
And because of the part where nothing exists we have
the use of a carriage wheel.
Clay is moulded into vessels,
And because of the space where nothing exists we are
able to use them as vessels.
Doors and windows are cut out in the walls of a
house,
And because they are empty spaces, we are able to use
them.
Therefore, on the one hand we have the benefit of
existence, and on the other, we make use of non-
existence.

CHAPTER 12

The five colours will blind a man's sight.
The five sounds will deaden a man's hearing.
The five tastes will spoil a man's palate.
Chasing and hunting will drive a man wild
Things hard to get will do harm to a man's
    conduct.
Therefore the Sage makes provision for the
    stomach and not for the eye.
He rejects the latter and chooses the former.

CHAPTER 13

'Favour and disgrace are like fear; fortune and disaster are like our body.'[1]

What does it mean by 'Favour and disgrace are like fear'? Favour is in a higher place, and disgrace in a lower place. When you win them you are like being in fear, and when you lose them you are also like being in fear. So favour and disgrace are like fear.[2]

What does it mean by 'Fortune and disaster are like our body'? We have fortune and disaster because we have a body. When we have no body, how can fortune or disaster befall us?

Therefore he who regards the world as he does the fortune of his own body can govern the world. He who loves the world as he does his own body can be entrusted with the world.

CHAPTER 14

That which we look at and cannot see is called
  plainness.
That which we listen to and cannot hear is called
  rareness.
That which we grope for and cannot get is called
  minuteness.
These three cannot be closely examined;
So they blend into One.
Revealed, it is not dazzling;
Hidden, it is not dark.
Infinite, it cannot be defined.
It goes back to non-existence.
It is called the form of the formless,
And the image of non-existence.
It is called mystery.
Meet it, you cannot see its face;
Follow it, you cannot see its back.[1]

By adhering to the Tao of the past
You will master the existence of the present
And be able to know the origin of the past.[2]
This is called the clue of Tao.

CHAPTER 15

In old times the perfect man of Tao[1] was subtle, penetrating and so profound that he can hardly be understood. Because he cannot be understood, I shall endeavour to picture him:

> He is cautious, like one who crosses a stream in winter;
> He is hesitating, like one who fears his neighbours;
> He is modest, like one who is a guest;
> He is yielding, like ice that is going to melt;
> He is simple, like wood that is not yet wrought;
> He is vacant, like valleys that are hollow;
> He is dim, like water that is turbid.

Who is able to purify the dark till it becomes slowly light?

Who is able to calm the turbid till it slowly clears?

Who is able to quicken the stagnant till it slowly makes progress?

He who follows these principles does not desire fullness.

Because he is not full, therefore when he becomes decayed he can renew.

CHAPTER 16

Attain to the goal of absolute vacuity;
Keep to the state of perfect peace.
All things come into existence,
And thence we see them return.
Look at the things that have been flourishing;
Each goes back to its origin.
Going back to the origin is called peace;
It means reversion to destiny.
Reversion to destiny is called eternity.
He who knows eternity is called enlightened.[1]
He who does not know eternity is running blindly
   into miseries.
Knowing eternity he is all-embracing.
Being all-embracing he can attain magnanimity.
Being magnanimous he can attain omnipresence.[2]
Being omnipresent he can attain supremacy.[3]
Being supreme he can attain Tao.
He who attains Tao is everlasting.
Though his body may decay he never perishes.

CHAPTER 17

The great rulers – the people do not[1] notice their
   existence;
The lesser ones – they attach to and praise them;
The still lesser ones – they fear them;
The still lesser ones – they despise them.
For where faith is lacking,
It cannot be met by faith.
Now how much importance must be attributed to
   words![2]

CHAPTER 18

When the great Tao is lost, spring forth benevolence
and righteousness.

When wisdom and sagacity arise, there are great
hypocrites.

When family relations are no longer harmonious, we
have filial children and devoted parents.

When a nation is in confusion and disorder, patriots
are recognized.

Where Tao is, equilibrium is. When Tao is lost, out
come all the differences of things.

CHAPTER 19

Do away with learning, and grief will not be known.[1]

Do away with sageness and eject wisdom, and the people will be more benefited a hundred times.

Do away with benevolence and eject righteousness, and the people will return to filial duty and parental love.

Do away with artifice and eject gains, and there will be no robbers and thieves.

These four, if we consider them as culture, are not sufficient.

Therefore let there be what the people can resort to:

Appear in plainness and hold to simplicity;

Restrain selfishness and curtail desires.

CHAPTER 20

Between yea and nay, how much difference is
    there?
Between good and evil, how much difference is
    there?
What are feared by others we must fear;
Vastly are they unlimited!
The people in general are as happy as if enjoying a
    great feast.
Or, as going up a tower in spring.
I alone am tranquil, and have made no signs,
Like a baby who is yet unable to smile;
Forlorn as if I had no home to go to.
Others all have more than enough,
And I alone seem to be in want.
Possibly mine is the mind of a fool,
Which is so ignorant!
The vulgar are bright,
And I alone seem to be dull.
The vulgar are discriminative, and I alone seem
    blunt.
I am negligent as if being obscure;[1]
Drifting, as if being attached to nothing.
The people in general all have something to do,
And I alone seem to be impractical and awkward.
I alone am different from others.
But I value seeking sustenance from the Mother.

CHAPTER 21

The great virtue as manifested is but following Tao.
Tao is a thing that is both invisible and intangible.
Intangible and invisible, yet there are forms in it;
Invisible and intangible, yet there is substance in it;
Subtle and obscure, there is essence in it;
This essence being invariably true, there is faith in
    it.
From of old till now, it has never lost its (nameless)
    name,
Through which the origin of all things has passed.
How do I know that it is so with the origin of all
    things?
By this (Tao).

CHAPTER 22

'Be humble, and you will remain entire.'
Be bent, and you will remain straight.
Be vacant, and you will remain full.
Be worn, and you will remain new.
He who has little will receive.
He who has much will be embarrassed.
Therefore the Sage keeps to One and becomes the
standard for the world.
He does not display himself; therefore he shines.
He does not approve himself; therefore he is noted.
He does not praise himself; therefore he has merit.
He does not glory in himself; therefore he excels.
And because he does not compete; therefore no one in
the world can compete with him.
The ancient saying 'Be humble and you will remain
entire' –
Can this be regarded as mere empty words?
Indeed he shall return home entire.

CHAPTER 23

To be sparing of words is natural.

A violent wind cannot last a whole morning; pelting rain cannot last a whole day. Who have made these things but heaven and earth? Inasmuch as heaven and earth cannot last for ever, how can man? He who engages himself in Tao is identified with Tao. He who engages himself in virtue is identified with virtue. He who engages himself in abandonment is identified with abandonment. Identified with Tao he will be well received by Tao. Identified with virtue he will be well received by virtue. Identified with abandonment he will be well received by abandonment.[1]

CHAPTER 24

A man on tiptoe cannot stand firm;
A man astride cannot walk on;
A man who displays himself cannot shine;
A man who approves himself cannot be noted;
A man who praises himself cannot have merit;
A man who glories in himself cannot excel:
These, when compared with Tao, are called;
'Excess in food and overdoing in action.'
Even in other things, mostly, they are rejected;
Therefore the man of Tao does not stay with them.

CHAPTER 25

There is a thing inherent and natural,
Which existed before heaven and earth.
Motionless and fathomless,
It stands alone and never changes;
It pervades everywhere and never becomes exhausted.
It may be regarded as the Mother of the Universe.
I do not know its name.
If I am forced to give it a name,
I call it Tao, and I name it as supreme.[1]
Supreme means going on;
Going on means going far;
Going far means returning.
Therefore Tao is supreme; heaven is supreme; earth is
     supreme; and man[2] is also supreme. There are in the
     universe four things supreme, and man is one of
     them.
Man follows the laws of earth;
Earth follows the laws of heaven;
Heaven follows the laws of Tao;
Tao follows the laws of its intrinsic nature.

CHAPTER 26

Heaviness is the basis of lightness;
Calmness is the controlling power of hastiness.
Therefore the Sage, though travelling all day long,
Never separates from his baggage-wagon;
Though surrounded with magnificent sights,
He lives in tranquillity.
How is it, then, that a king of ten thousand chariots
Should conduct himself so lightly in the empire?
To be light is to lose the basis;
To be hasty is to lose the controlling power.

CHAPTER 27

A good traveller leaves no track;
A good speaker leaves no error;
A good reckoner needs no counter;
A good closer needs no bars or bolts,
And yet it is impossible to open after him.
A good fastener needs no cords or knots,
And yet it is impossible to untie after him.[1]
Even if men be bad, why should they be rejected?[2]
Therefore the Sage is always a good saviour of men,
And no man is rejected;
He is a good saviour of things,
And nothing is rejected:
This is called double enlightenment.
Therefore good men are bad men's instructors,
And bad men are good men's materials.
Those who do not esteem their instructors,
And those who do not love their materials,
Though expedient, are in fact greatly confused.
This is essential subtlety.

CHAPTER 28

He who knows the masculine and yet keeps to the
feminine
Will become a channel drawing all the world towards
it;
Being a channel of the world, he will not be severed
from the eternal virtue,
And then he can return again to the state of infancy.
He who knows the white and yet keeps to the black
Will become the standard of the world;
Being the standard of the world, with him eternal
virtue will never falter,
And then he can return again to the absolute.
He who knows honour and yet keeps to humility
Will become a valley that receives all the world into it;
Being a valley of the world, with him eternal virtue will
be complete,
And then he can return again to wholeness.
Wholeness, when divided, will make vessels of utility;
These when employed by the Sage will become
officials and chiefs.
However, for a great function no discrimination is
needed.

CHAPTER 29

When a man is to take the world over and shape it,
I see that he must be obliged to do it.[1]
For the world is a divine vessel:
It cannot be shaped;[2]
Nor can it be insisted upon.
He who shapes it damages it;
He who insists upon it loses it.
Therefore the Sage does not shape it, so he does not
    damage it;
He does not insist upon it, so he does not lose it.[3]
For, among all things, some go ahead, while others lag
    behind;
Some keep their mouth shut, while others give forth
    puffs;
Some are strong, while others are weak;
Some are on the cart, while others fall off.
Therefore the Sage avoids excess, extravagance and
    indulgence.

CHAPTER 30

He who assists a ruler of men with Tao does not force
the world with arms.[1]

He aims only at carrying out relief, and does not
venture to force his power upon others.

When relief is done, he will not be assuming,

He will not be boastful; he will not be proud;

And he will think that he was obliged to do it.

So it comes that relief is done without resorting to
force.

When things come to the summit of their vigour,
they begin to grow old.

This is against Tao.

What is against Tao will soon come to an end.

CHAPTER 31

So far[1] as arms are concerned, they are implements of ill-omen.[2] They are not implements for the man of Tao. For the actions of arms will be well requited; where armies have been quartered brambles and thorns grow. Great wars are for certain followed by years of scarcity. The man of Tao when dwelling at home makes the left as the place of honour, and when using arms makes the right as the place of honour. He uses them only when he cannot avoid it. In his conquests he takes no delight. If he take delight in them, it would mean that he enjoys in the slaughter of men. He who takes delight in the slaughter of men cannot have his will done in the world.

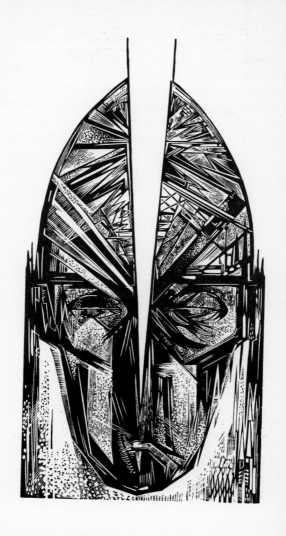

CHAPTER 32

Tao was always nameless.[1]
When for the first time applied to function, it was
    named.
Inasmuch as names are given, one should also know
    where to stop.
Knowing where to stop one can become imperishable.[2]

CHAPTER 33

He who knows others is wise;
He who knows himself is enlightened.
He who conquers others is strong;
He who conquers himself is mighty.
He who knows contentment is rich.
He who keeps on his course with energy has will.
He who does not deviate from his proper place will
   long endure.
He who may die but not perish has longevity.[1]

CHAPTER 34

The great Tao pervades everywhere, both on the left and on the right.

By it all things came into being, and it does not reject them.

Merits accomplished, it does not possess them.

It loves and nourishes all things but does not dominate over them.

It is always non-existent; therefore it can be named as small.

All things return home to it, and it does not claim mastery over them; therefore it can be named as great.

Because it never assumes greatness, therefore it can accomplish greatness.

CHAPTER 35

To him who holds to the Great Form[1] all the world will
    go.
It will go and see no danger, but tranquillity, equality
    and community.
Music and dainties will make the passing stranger
    stop.
But Tao when uttered in words is so pure and void of
    flavour
When one looks at it, one cannot see it;
When one listens to it, one cannot hear it.
However, when one uses it, it is inexhaustible.[2]

CHAPTER 36

In order to contract a thing, one should surely expand
    it first.
In order to weaken, one will surely strengthen first.
In order to overthrow, one will surely exalt first.[1]
'In order to take, one will surely give first.'
This is called subtle wisdom.
The soft and weak can overcome the hard and strong.
As the fish should not leave the deep
So should the sharp implements of a nation not be
    shown to anyone.[2]

CHAPTER 37

Tao is ever inactive, and yet there is nothing that it does not do.

If princes and kings could keep to it, all things would of themselves become developed.

When they are developed, desire would stir in them;

I would restrain them by the nameless Simplicity,[1]

In order to make them free from desire.

Free from desire, they would be at rest;

And the world would of itself become rectified.

However insignificant Simplicity seems, the whole world cannot make it submissive.

If princes and kings could keep to it,

All things in the world would of themselves pay homage.

Heaven and earth would unite to send down sweet dew.

The people with no one to command them would of themselves become harmonious.[2]

When merits are accomplished and affairs completed,

The people would speak of themselves as following nature.[3]

CHAPTER 38

The superior virtue is not conscious of itself as virtue;
Therefore it has virtue.
The inferior virtue never lets off virtue;
Therefore it has no virtue.
The superior virtue seems inactive, and yet there is
nothing that it does not do.
The inferior virtue acts and yet in the end leaves things
undone.
The superior benevolence acts without a motive.
The superior righteousness acts with a motive.
The superior ritual acts, but at first no one responds to
it;
Gradually people raise their arms and follow it.
Therefore when Tao is lost, virtue follows.
When virtue is lost, benevolence follows.
When benevolence is lost, righteousness follows.
When righteousness is lost, ritual follows.
Ritual, therefore, is the attenuation of loyalty and faith
and the outset of confusion.
Fore-knowledge is the flower of Tao and the
beginning of folly.
Therefore the truly great man keeps to the solid and
not to the tenuous;
Keeps to the fruit and not to the flower.
Thus he rejects the latter and takes the former.

CHAPTER 39

From of old the things that have acquired Unity are
these:
Heaven by Unity has become clear;
Earth by Unity has become steady;
The Spirit by Unity has become spiritual;
The Valley by Unity has become full;
All things by Unity have come into existence;
Princes and kings by Unity have become rulers of the
world.[1]
If heaven were not clear, it would be rent;
If earth were not steady, it would be tumbled down;
If the Spirit[2] were not active, it would pass away;
If the Valley[2] were not full, it would be dried up;
If all things were not existing, they would be extinct;
If princes and kings were not rulers, they would be
overthrown.
The noble must be styled in the terms of the humble;
The high must take the low as their foundation.
Therefore princes and kings call themselves 'the
ignorant', 'the virtueless' and 'the unworthy'.
Does this not mean that they take the humble as their
root?
What men hate most are 'the ignorant', 'the
virtueless' and 'the unworthy'.
And yet princes and kings choose them as their titles.[3]

Therefore the highest fame is to have no fame.
Thus kings are increased by being diminished;
They are diminished by being increased.
It is undesirable to be as prominent as a single gem,
Or as monotonously numerous as stones.

CHAPTER 40

Returning is the motion of Tao,[1]
Weakness is the appliance of Tao.[2]
All things in the Universe come from existence,
And existence from non-existence.

CHAPTER 41

When the superior scholar is told of Tao,
He works hard to practise it.
When the middling scholar is told of Tao,
It seems that sometimes he keeps it and sometimes he
  loses it.
When the inferior scholar is told of Tao,
He laughs aloud at it.
If it were not laughed at, it would not be sufficient to
  be Tao.
Therefore the proverb says:
'Tao in enlightenment seems obscure;
Tao in progress seems regressive;
Tao in its straightness seems rugged.
The highest virtue seems like a valley;
The purest white seems discoloured;
The most magnificent virtue seems insufficient;
The solidest virtue seems frail;
The simplest nature seems changeable;
The greatest square has no angles;
The largest vessel is never complete;
The loudest sound can scarcely be heard;
The biggest form cannot be visualized.
Tao, while hidden, is nameless.'
Yet it is Tao alone that is good at imparting and
  completing.

CHAPTER 42

Tao begets One; one begets two; two begets three; three begets all things.[1] All things are backed by the Shade (yin) and faced by the Light (yang), and harmonized by the immaterial Breath (ch'i).[2]

What others teach, I also teach: 'The daring and violent do not die a natural death.' This (maxim) I shall regard as my instructor.

CHAPTER 43

The non-existent can enter into the impenetrable.[1]
By this I know that non-action is useful.
Teaching without words, utility without action –
Few in the world have come to this.

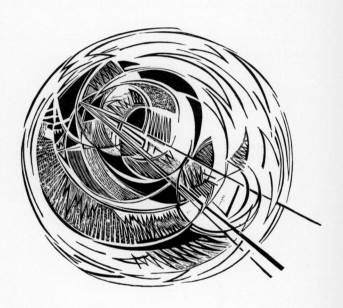

CHAPTER 44

Fame or your person, which is nearer to you?
Your person or wealth, which is dearer to you?
Gain or loss, which brings more evil to you?
Over-love of anything will lead to wasteful spending;
Amassed riches will be followed by heavy plundering.
Therefore, he who knows contentment can never be
    humiliated;
He who knows[1] where to stop can never be perishable;
He will long endure.

CHAPTER 45

The greatest perfection seems imperfect;
Yet its use will last without decay.
The greatest fullness seems empty;
Yet its use cannot be exhausted.
The greatest straightness seems crooked;
The greatest dexterity seems awkward;
The greatest eloquence seems[1] stammering.
Activity overcomes cold;
Quietness overcomes heat.
Only through purity and quietude can the world be
   ruled.

CHAPTER 46

When Tao reigns in the world
Swift horses are curbed for hauling the dung-carts (in
the field).
When Tao does not reign in the world,
War horses are bred on the commons (outside the
cities).
There is no greater crime than seeking what men
desire;[1]
There is no greater misery than knowing no content;
There is no greater calamity than indulging in greed.
Therefore the contentment of knowing content will
ever be contented.

CHAPTER 47

Without going out of the door
One can know the whole world;
Without peeping out of the window
One can see the Tao of heaven.
The further one travels
The less one knows.
Therefore the Sage knows everything without
   travelling;
He names everything without seeing it;
He accomplishes everything without doing it.

CHAPTER 48

He who pursues learning will increase every day;
He who pursues Tao will decrease every day.[1]
He will decrease and continue to decrease,
Till he comes to non-action;
By non-action everything can be done.[2]

CHAPTER 49

The Sage has no self (to call his own);
He makes the self of the people his self.
To the good I act with goodness;
To the bad I also act with goodness:
Thus goodness is attained.
To the faithful I act with faith;
To the faithless I also act with faith:
Thus faith is attained.
The Sage lives in the world in concord, and rules over
   the world in simplicity.
Yet what all the people turn their ears and eyes to,[1]
The Sage looks after as a mother does her children.

CHAPTER 50

Men go out of life and enter into death.

The parts (proportions) of life are three in ten; the parts of death are also three in ten. Men that from birth move towards the region of death are also three in ten. Why is it so? Because of their redundant effort in seeking to live. But only those who do nothing for the purpose of living are better than those who prize their lives.[1] For I have heard that he who knows well how to conserve life, when travelling on land, does not meet the rhinoceros or the tiger; when going to a battle he is not attacked by arms and weapons. The rhinoceros can find nowhere to drive his horn; the tiger can find nowhere to put his claws; the weapons can find nowhere to thrust their blades. Why is it so? Because he is beyond the region of death.

CHAPTER 51

Tao produces them (all things);
Virtue feeds them;
All of them appear in different forms;
Each is perfected by being given power.
Therefore none of the numerous things does not
honour Tao and esteem virtue.
The honouring of Tao and the esteem of virtue are
done, not by command, but always of their own
accord.
Therefore Tao produces them, makes them grow,
nourishes them, shelters them, brings them up and
protects them.
When all things come into being Tao does not reject
them.
It produces them without holding possession of them.
It acts without depending upon them, and raises
without lording it over them.
When merits are accomplished it does not lay claim to
them.
Because it does not lay claim to them, therefore it does
not lose them.

CHAPTER 52

The beginning of the Universe, when manifested, may
    be regarded as its Mother.
When a man has found the Mother, he will know the
    children accordingly;
Though he has known the children, he still keeps to the
    Mother:
Thus, however his body may decay, he will never
    perish.
If he shuts his mouth and closes his doors,
He can never be exhausted.
If he opens his mouth and increases his affairs,
He can never be saved.
To see the minuteness of things is called clarity of
    sight;
To keep to what is weak is called power.
Use your light, but dim your brightness;
Thus you will cause no harm to yourself.
This is called following the eternal (Tao).

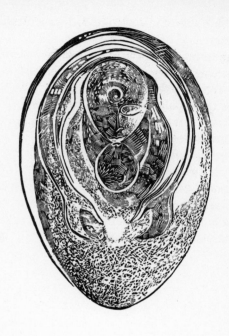

CHAPTER 53

Let me have sound knowledge and walk on the great
    way (Tao);
Only I am in fear of deviating.
The great way is very plain and easy,
But the people prefer by-paths.
While the royal palaces are very well kept,
The fields are left weedy
And the granaries empty.
To wear embroidered clothes,
To carry sharp swords,
To be satiated in drink and food,
To be possessed of redundant riches –
This is called encouragement to robbery.
Is it not deviating[1] from Tao?

CHAPTER 54

What is planted by the best planter can never be
    removed;
What is embraced by the best embracer can never be
    loosened.
Thus his children and grandchildren will be able to
    continue their ancestral sacrifice for endless
    generations.
If he applies Tao to himself his virtue will be genuine;
If he applies it to his family his virtue will be abundant;
If he applies it to his village his virtue will be lasting;
If he applies it to his country his virtue will be full;
If he applies it to the world his virtue will be universal.
Therefore by one's person one may observe persons;
By one's family one may observe families;
By one's village one may observe villages;
By one's country one may observe countries;
By one's world one may observe worlds.
How do I know that the world may be so (governed by
    Tao)?
By this (observation).

CHAPTER 55

He who is endowed with ample virtue may be
   compared to an infant.
No venomous insects sting him;
Nor fierce beasts seize him;
Nor birds of prey strike him.[1]
His bones are frail, his sinews tender, but his grasp is
   strong.
He does not know the conjugation of male and female,
   and yet he has sexual development;
It means he is in the best vitality.
He may cry all day long without growing hoarse;
It means that he is in the perfect harmony.
To know this harmony is to approach eternity;
To know eternity is to attain enlightenment.
To increase life is to lead to calamity;
To let the heart exert the breath is to become stark.[2]

CHAPTER 56

Blunt all that is sharp;[1]
Cut all that is divisible;[2]
Blur all that is brilliant;
Mix with all that is humble as dust;
This is called absolute equality.
Therefore it cannot be made intimate;
Nor can it be alienated.
It cannot be benefited;
Nor can it be harmed.
It cannot be exalted;
Nor can it be debased.
Therefore it is the most valuable thing in the world.

CHAPTER 57

Albeit one governs the country by rectitude,
And carries on wars by stratagems,
Yet one must rule the empire by meddling with no
business.
The empire can always be ruled by meddling with no
business.
Otherwise, it can never be done.[1]
How do I know it is so?
By this:[2]
The more restrictions and avoidances are in the
empire,
The poorer become the people;
The more sharp implements the people keep,
The more confusions are in the country;
The more arts and crafts men have,
The more are fantastic things produced;
The more laws and regulations are given,
The more robbers and thieves there are.
Therefore the Sage says;
Inasmuch as I betake myself to non-action, the people
of themselves become developed.
Inasmuch as I love quietude, the people of themselves
become righteous.
Inasmuch as I make no fuss, the people of themselves
become wealthy.
Inasmuch as I am free from desire, the people of
themselves remain simple.

CHAPTER 58

When the government is blunt and inactive the
    people will be happy and prosperous;
When the government is discriminative, the people
    will be dissatisfied and restless.
It is upon misery that happiness rests;
It is under happiness that misery lies.
Who then can know the supremacy (good government)?
Only when the government does no rectifying.
Otherwise, rectitude will again become stratagem,
And good become evil.
Men have been ignorant of this, since long ago.
Therefore the Sage is square but does not cut others;
He is angled but does not chip others;
He is straight but does not stretch others;
He is bright but does not dazzle others.

CHAPTER 59

In ruling men and in serving Heaven, the Sage uses only moderation.

By moderation alone he is able to have conformed early (to Tao).

This early conformity is called intensive accumulation of virtue.

With this intensive accumulation of virtue, there is nothing that he cannot overcome.

Because there is nothing that he cannot overcome, no one will be able to know his supremacy.

Because no one knows his supremacy he can take possession of a country.

Because what he does is identified with the Mother in taking possession of a country, he can long endure.

This means that he is deep rooted and firmly based, and knows the way of longevity and immortality.

CHAPTER 60

Govern a great state as you would cook a small fish (do
   it gently).
Let Tao reign over the world, and no spirits will show
   their ghostly powers.
Not that the spirits have no more powers,
But their powers will not harm men.
Neither will they harm men,
Nor will the Sage harm the people.[1]
Inasmuch as none of them harms anybody,
Therefore virtue belongs to them both.

CHAPTER 61

A great state is the world's low-stream (to which all the river flows down), the world's field and the world's female. The female always conquers the male by quietude, which is employed as a means to lower oneself. Thus a great state lowers itself towards a small state before it takes over the small state. A small state lowers itself towards a great state before it takes over the great state. Therefore some lower themselves to take, while others lower themselves to gather. A great state wishes nothing more than to have and keep many people, and a small state wishes nothing more than to get more things to do. When the two both mean to obtain their wishes, the greater one should lower itself.

CHAPTER 62

Tao is the source of all things, the treasure of good men, and the sustainer of bad men.[1]

Therefore at the enthronement of an emperor and the appointment of the three ministers, better still than those, who present jewels followed by horses, is the one who sitting presents (propounds) this Tao. Why did the ancients prize this Tao? Was it not because it could be attained by seeking and thus sinners could be freed? For this reason it has become the most valuable thing in the world.

Good words will procure one honour; good deeds will get one credit.

CHAPTER 63

Act non-action; undertake no undertaking; taste the
tasteless.

The Sage desires the desireless, and prizes no articles
that are difficult to get.

He learns no learning, but reviews what others have
passed through.

Thus he lets all things develop in their natural way,
and does not venture to act.

Regard the small as great; regard the few as many.

Manage the difficult while they are easy;

Manage the great while they are small.

All difficult things in the world start from the easy;

All great things in the world start from the small.

The tree that fills a man's arms arises from a tender
shoot;

The nine-storeyed tower is raised from a heap of earth;

A thousand miles' journey begins from the spot under
one's feet.

Therefore the Sage never attempts great things, and
thus he can achieve what is great.

He who makes easy promises will seldom keep his
word;

He who regards many things as easy will find many
difficulties.

Therefore the Sage regards things as difficult, and
consequently never has difficulties.

CHAPTER 64

What is motionless is easy to hold;
What is not yet foreshadowed is easy to form plans for;
What is fragile is easy to break;
What is minute is easy to disperse.
Deal with a thing before it comes into existence;
Regulate a thing before it gets into confusion.
The common people in their business often fail on the
    verge of succeeding.
Take care with the end as you do with the beginning,
And you will have no failure.

CHAPTER 65

In olden times the best practisers of Tao did not use it
   to awaken the people to knowledge,
But used it to restore them to simplicity.
People are difficult to govern because they have much
   knowledge.
Therefore to govern the country by increasing the
   people's knowledge is to be the destroyer of the
   country;
To govern the country by decreasing their knowledge
   is to be the blesser of the country.
To be acquainted with these two ways is to know the
   standard;
To keep the standard always in mind is to have sublime
   virtue.
Sublime virtue is infinitely deep and wide.
It goes reverse to all things;
And so it attains perfect peace.

CHAPTER 66

As Tao is to the world so are streams and valleys to
 rivers and seas.[1]
Rivers and seas can be kings to all valleys because the
 former can well lower themselves to the latter.
Thus they become kings to all valleys.
Therefore the Sage, in order to be above the people,
 must in words keep below them;
In order to be ahead of the people, he must in person
 keep behind them.
Thus when he is above, the people do not feel his
 burden;
When he is ahead, the people do not feel his
 hindrance.
Therefore all the world is pleased to hold him in high
 esteem and never get tired of him.
Because he does not compete; therefore no one
 competes with him.

CHAPTER 67

All the world says to me: 'Great as Tao is, it resembles no description (form).' Because it is great, therefore it resembles no description. If it resembled any description it would have long since become small.[1]

I have three treasures, which I hold and keep safe:

The first is called love;

The second is called moderation;

The third is called not venturing to go ahead of the world.

Being loving, one can be brave;[2]

Being moderate, one can be ample;

Not venturing to go ahead of the world,[2] one can be the chief of all officials.

Instead of love, one has only bravery;

Instead of moderation, one has only amplitude;

Instead of keeping behind, one goes ahead:

These lead to nothing but death.

For he who fights with love will win the battle;

He who defends with love will be secure.

Heaven will save him, and protect him with love.

CHAPTER 68

The best soldier is not soldierly;
The best fighter is not ferocious;
The best conqueror does not take part in war;
The best employer of men keeps himself below them.
This is called the virtue of not contending;
This is called the ability of using men;
This is called the supremacy of consorting with heaven.

CHAPTER 69

An ancient[1] tactician has said:

'I dare not act as a host but would rather act as a guest;[2]

I dare not advance an inch but would rather retreat a foot.'

This implies that he does not marshal the ranks as if there were no ranks;

He does not roll up his sleeves as if he had no arms;

He does not seize as if he had no weapons;

He does not fight as if there were no enemies.

No calamity is greater than under-estimating the enemy.

To under-estimate the enemy is to be on the point of losing our treasure (love).

Therefore when opposing armies meet in the field the ruthful will win.

CHAPTER 70

Words have an ancestor; deeds have a governor.[1]

My words are very easy to know, and very easy to practise,

Yet all men in the world do not know them, nor do they practise them.

It is because they have[2] knowledge that they do not know me.

When those who know me are few, eventually I am beyond all praise.

Therefore the Sage wears clothes of coarse cloth but carries jewels in his bosom;

He knows himself but does not display himself;

He loves himself but does not hold himself in high esteem.

Thus he rejects the latter and takes the former.

CHAPTER 71

Not knowing that one knows is best;
Thinking that one knows when one does not know is
  sickness.
Only when one becomes sick of this sickness can one
  be free from sickness.
The Sage is never sick; because he is sick of this
  sickness, therefore he is not sick.

CHAPTER 72

If the people have no fear of their ruling authority,
    still greater fear will come.
Be sure not to give them too narrow a dwelling;
Nor make their living scanty.
Only when their dwelling place is no longer narrow
    will their dissatisfaction come to an end.

CHAPTER 73

He who shows courage in daring will perish;
He who shows courage in not-daring will live.
To know these two is to distinguish the one, benefit,
from the other, harm.
Who can tell that one of them should be loathed by
heaven?[1]
The Tao of heaven does not contend; yet it surely
wins the victory.
It does not speak; yet it surely responds.
It does not call; yet all things come of their own
accord.
It remains taciturn; yet it surely makes plans.
The net of heaven is vast, and its meshes are wide;
Yet from it nothing escapes.

CHAPTER 74

When the people are not afraid of death, what use is it to frighten them with the punishment of death? If the people were constantly afraid of death and we could arrest and kill those who commit treacheries, who then would dare to commit such? Only the Supreme Executioner kills. To kill in place of the Supreme Executioner is to hack instead of a greater carpenter. Now if one hacks in place of a great carpenter one can scarcely avoid cutting one's own hand.

CHAPTER 75

The people starve. Because their officials take heavy taxes from them, therefore they starve. The people are hard to rule. Because their officials meddle with affairs, therefore they are hard to rule. The people pay no heed to death. Because they endeavour to seek life; therefore they pay no heed to death.[1]

CHAPTER 76

Man when living is soft and tender; when dead he is hard and tough. All animals and plants when living are tender and fragile; when dead they become withered and dry. Therefore it is said: the hard and tough are parts of death; the soft and tender are parts of life. This is the reason why the soldiers when they are too tough cannot carry the day; the tree when it is too tough will break.[1] The position of the strong and great is low, and the position of the weak and tender is high.

CHAPTER 77

Is not the Tao of heaven like the drawing of a bow? It brings down the part which is high; it raises the part which is low; it lessens the part which is redundant (convex); it fills up the part which is insufficient (concave). The Tao of heaven is to lessen the redundant and fill up the insufficient. The Tao of man, on the contrary, is to take from the insufficient and give to the redundant.[1] Who can take from the redundant and give to the insufficient? Only he who has Tao can.[2] Therefore the Sage does not hoard. The more he helps others, the more he benefits himself; the more he gives to others, the more he gets himself. The Tao of heaven does one good but never does one harm; the Tao of the Sage acts but never contends.[3]

CHAPTER 78

The weakest things in the world can overmatch the
strongest things in the world.[1]

Nothing in the world can be compared to water for its
weak and yielding nature; yet in attacking the hard
and the strong nothing proves better than it. For
there is no other alternative to it.

The weak can overcome the strong and the yielding
can overcome the hard:

This all the world knows but does not practise.

Therefore the Sage says:

He who sustains all the reproaches of the country can
be the master of the land;

He who sustains all the calamities of the country can
be the king of the world.

These are words of truth,

Though they seem paradoxical.

CHAPTER 79

Return love for great hatred.[1]
Otherwise, when a great hatred is reconciled, some of
  it will surely remain.
How can this end in goodness?
Therefore the Sage holds to the left half[2] of an
  agreement but does not exact what the other holder
  ought to do.
The virtuous resort to agreement;
The virtueless resort to exaction.
'The Tao of heaven shows no partiality;
It abides always with good men.'

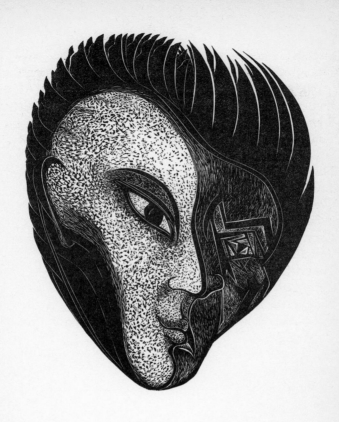

CHAPTER 80

Supposing here is a small state with few people.

Though there are various vessels I will not have them
put in use.

I will make the people regard death as a grave matter
and not go far away.

Though they have boats and carriages they will not
travel in them;

Though they have armour and weapons they will not
show them.

I will let them restore the use of knotted cords
(instead of writing).

They will be satisfied with their food;

Delighted in their dress;

Comfortable in their dwellings;

Happy with their customs.

Though the neighbouring states are within sight

And their cocks' crowing and dogs' barking within
hearing;

The people (of the small state) will not go there all
their lives.

CHAPTER 81

He who knows does not speak;
He who speaks does not know.[1]
He who is truthful is not showy;
He who is showy is not truthful.
He who is virtuous does not dispute;
He who disputes is not virtuous;
He who is learned is not wise;
He who is wise is not learned.[2]
Therefore the Sage does not display his own merits.[3]

NOTES

CHAPTER 1

1 The eternal Tao cannot be put into words, nor can the unchanging name be given a definition; for words are but symbols and a definition is based upon the relativity of things. How can they represent the all-embracing, true Tao and the nameless name? So only for the convenience of speaking we call it Tao (cf. Chapter 25). But nevertheless it is ever unchanging, the same, and profound.

2 Non-existence is not equal to nought or nothingness, but a state before existence comes into being (cf. Chapters 4, 21 and 25).

3 'Profundity' is a rendering of the Chinese word hsuan 玄, which means (literally a small thing covered by a man) the minuteness of the Universe not yet discovered by man. 'Infinite profundity' is 玄之又玄 literally 'profundity in profundity' or 'minuteness in minuteness'. This might be said to imply the rudiment of the modern scientific and philosophical theories of atom, electron, quantum hypothesis, etc.

CHAPTER 2

Everything in the Universe, when defined, is relative to every other thing. What the Sage should do is not to try to distinguish things nor show his preference for any, either by making efforts or by giving demonstrations. This does not mean that he does nothing or speaks nothing at all, but that he takes things as they are, with ease, and naturally, and makes no fuss about them.

1 The rest of this chapter, according to Prof. Ma Hsü-lun, should belong to Chapter 51, which see.

CHAPTER 3

The restlessness and disorderliness of the world are caused by the ambitious who strive to get to what is lofty, and the cunning who go from what is undesirable to what is desirable. If the rulers of the world keep, as the Sage does, their people's body and soul always balanced, the world's peace will be preserved.

CHAPTER 4

This chapter devotes itself to the discussion of the nature of Tao. As it has been said in Chapter 1 that Tao cannot be properly expressed, here again no definite assertions are made. Note the words 'likely', 'seems' and 'looks like'; from these analogies one can get some notion of the nature of Tao, but still cannot tell exactly what Tao itself is (cf. Chapter 25). The middle part of this chapter (as found in other translations) goes to Chapter 56.

CHAPTER 5

1 The 'straw-dog', according to Chuang Tzu, is an image for sacrifice, and he says (*Chuang Tzu,* XIV): 'The straw-dog, before it is used, is kept in a box, covered with silk and offered with proper ceremony. When it has been used, those who walk by step upon its head and back, and the grass-gatherer takes it and burns it in the fire.' In like manner heaven and earth leave the innumerable creatures to come into being, grow and die away all of their own accord, and the Sage regards his people in the same way. Since natural evolution is not the doing of heaven and earth nor of the Sage, it is proper not to assume the credit to themselves. Likewise the innumerable creatures have their lives, activities and accomplishments all spontaneously, which it is not in their power to undo and which they should not dwell upon. For this is Tao (cf. Chapter 34).

2 Within the hollowness of heaven and earth all creatures are contained. Owing to the creatures' moving in it, more and more of them are produced.

3 Confucius said: 'Does Heaven speak? The four seasons pursue their courses, and all things are continually being produced, but does Heaven say anything?' (*Analects,* XVII, 19).

The last two passages do not seem relevant to this chapter; therefore they are put separately.

116

CHAPTER 6

The Valley (谷 ku) and the Spirit (神 shên) are the two formative elements in the Universe, 陰 yin and 陽 yang (female and male, negative and positive, etc.). They are mentioned again in Chapter 39.

CHAPTER 7

Although heaven and earth seem to have given life to all creatures, they do not strive for their self-existence, therefore they live long and never die. In ruling a state the Sage does all for the people in spite of his personal aims, and in the end he achieves merits, reputation and everything for himself.

CHAPTER 8

This is to show how the Sage, the personified form of highest good, is unselfish. He does good to others but does not contend with them. He has no spite for what others disdain. He is content with everything. With him as an example, the world would be at peace.

CHAPTER 10

The chapter is dealing with conservation of life, and it is fully expounded in *Chuang Tzu*, XXIII.

CHAPTER 11

Without space we cannot have the benefit of a carriage wheel, a vessel or a house. Without wooden spokes, clay moulds and walls we cannot make use of the space in them. Existence and non-existence, after all, are co-existent and interdependent.

CHAPTER 12

According to the ancient scheme of physics, on which many other theories were based, all things in the Universe are classified into five: thus the five colours are *blue, yellow,*

117

red, *white* and *black*; the five sounds (i.e. five tones in music) *do, re, mi, sol* and *la*; the five tastes *sweet, sour, bitter, pungent* and *salt*.

Compare this with Chapter 3.

CHAPTER 13

1 This is an old saying which Lao Tzu quotes and interprets, and from which he finally leads up to his own meaning.
2 Favour and disgrace are like fear, because they are distinguished as 'higher' and 'lower'. If favour were not regarded as favour and disgrace not as disgrace, there would be no fear at all. So are fortune and disaster with body. Cf. Chapter 7.

CHAPTER 14

1 Lines 1–14 treat of the nature of Tao. The last four lines do not seem to follow the idea quite well, so they are set apart.
2 As the present is to the past so is the past to the origin of the past.

CHAPTER 15

1 Instead of 士 shih or 天下 tien hsia, I follow Prof. Ma Hsü-lun's reading as 道 tao, which will include the sense of 'wise men', 'officers' or 'rulers'.

It is difficult to 'purify', 'calm' or 'quicken' things without producing unnecessary defects; only by doing it 'slowly' can perfection be attained.

CHAPTER 16

1 Before things come into existence their destiny is life; after they have flourished their destiny is death. Origin is where life and death meet – it is eternity.
2 王 read 周.
3 天 read 大.

CHAPTER 17

1 下 read 不.
2 Two lines under this go to Chapter 37.

CHAPTER 18

Cf. Chapter 2.

CHAPTER 19

1 The first line is from the beginning of next chapter.

This chapter, being a sequel to the last one, suggests a remedy for all the differences and disorders resulting from the loss of Tao.

CHAPTER 20

1 海 read 腼.

CHAPTER 21

Cf. Chapters 1, 4 and 14.

CHAPTER 23

This is the same idea as actionless business and wordless teaching (see end of Chapter 2 and note to Chapter 5).

Violent wind and pelting rain are not *always* and *naturally* so, therefore they cannot last long.

1 Two lines at the end are omitted, because they have appeared previously in Chapter 17 (lines 5 and 6).

CHAPTER 24

These are instances of living against Nature.

CHAPTER 25

1 大 etymologically shows a man stretching out both his hands and feet, and he cannot be greater than this; therefore it befits the meanings of *far-reaching* and *supreme*.

2 王 read 人.

CHAPTER 26

Wang Pi in his commentary says: 'The light cannot bear the heavy; the small cannot allay the great; those who do not travel control those who travel; those who do not move control those who move. Therefore, heaviness should be the basis of lightness and calmness the controlling power of hastiness.'

The last seven lines are from the beginning of Chapter 27.

CHAPTER 27

1 The first part seems to be an independent chapter. Cf. *Chuang Tzu*, III, first part.
2 The first line of the second part is from Chapter 62.

CHAPTER 28

Yen Fu commenting on this chapter says: 'He who keeps to the feminine, the black and humility must *know* the masculine, the white and honour. Otherwise, the feminine, the black and humility themselves are not valuable at all.'

Wholeness is the state of entirety and simplicity. Though, when cut and carved, it may serve lesser purposes, it then can no longer answer the purpose of great function, for which only wholeness itself is qualified.

CHAPTER 29

1 See *Chuang Tzu*, XI, beginning.
2 Wang Pi commenting on this line says: 'Everything has its own nature. It can be developed according to its nature, but not shaped or forced upon against it.'
3 Lines 8 and 9 are from Chapter 64.

CHAPTER 30

1 Two lines after this are transferred to next chapter.

CHAPTER 31

1 According to Wang Nien-sun, 佳 (chia) should be 隹 (chui) the old form of 唯 (wei).
2 Two lines after this have previously appeared at the end of Chapter 24, and therefore they are here omitted.

In many texts there is at the end of this chapter a passage which runs as follows:

'In auspicious affairs the place of honour is left; in adverse affairs the place of honour is right. The adjutant-general takes his place on the left; the general-in-chief takes his place on the right – it means that this is the order of funeral. A slaughter of many people is mourned with heavy grief. A victory in war is disposed according to a funeral.'

These words are too superficial to conform to the dignified style of the writing of Lao Tzu. Possibly they are old annotations affixed by a mistake to the text proper.

CHAPTER 32

1 Seven lines after this are shifted to the end of Chapter 37.
2 One line at the end goes to Chapter 66.

CHAPTER 33

Han Fei-tzu says: 'The difficulty of knowing does not lie in seeing others, but in seeing oneself. Therefore he who sees himself is enlightened.'

1 He cannot deviate from his place, because he becomes one with all things; he cannot perish, because he lives as long as heaven and earth.

CHAPTER 34

Cf. Chapters 1, 25 and 51.

CHAPTER 35

1 The Great Form is Tao itself, to which 'all things return home'. (See the foregoing chapter.)
2 Tao does not attract people as other things do; yet, 'in use it can never be exhausted'. (See Chapter 6.)

CHAPTER 36

1 Yen Fu says: 'Expansion, strengthening, and exaltation – all are "against Tao", and "will soon come to an end". (See end of Chapter 30.) Those who receive these should beware.'

2 Wang Pi says: 'Things should be developed according to their nature without the use of sharp implements. When implements are shown, all will be at a loss, just as fish have left water against Nature.'

CHAPTER 37

1 According to Lo Chên-yü, a tautological phrase 'nameless simplicity' is hereafter omitted.
2 The second part is from Chapter 32.
3 The last two lines are from Chapter 17.

CHAPTER 39

1 After line 7 there is in other texts a phrase 'These are all effects of Unity', which, according to Ma Hsü-Lun, is an old annotation.
2 Etymologically, Spirit (shên) comes from 申, meaning 'stretching', and Valley (ku) from ⼝, meaning 'a mouth or receptacle'; therefore Spirit and Valley here mean 'male and female'. (See Chapter 6, first line and note.)
3 Lines 18 and 19 are from Chapter 42.

CHAPTER 40

1 Cf. Chapters 16 and 25.
2 Cf. Chapter 28.

CHAPTER 41

Chuang Tzu says (in Chapter II): 'Separating is to be constructing; constructing is to be destroying. All things, regardless of their separation and construction, will again bring to the one.'

CHAPTER 42

1 Yen Fu says: 'Tao is the Primordial; it is absolute. In its descent it begets one. When one is begotten, Tao becomes relative, and two comes into existence. When two things are compared, there is their opposite, and three is begotten.'
2 Two lines after this have been removed to Chapter 39.

CHAPTER 43

1 One line before this goes to Chapter 78.

CHAPTER 44

1 Yen Fu says: 'It is vitally important to *know* contentment, and to *know* where to stop; otherwise, one cannot endure long.'

CHAPTER 45

1 Notice the word 'seems'; it denotes that 'imperfect', 'empty', etc., are not actually so, but the 'appliance of Tao'. (See Chapter 40.)

CHAPTER 46

1 This line is not in Wang Pi's text.

CHAPTER 47

Cf. the last four lines of Chapter 14 and Chapter 48.

CHAPTER 48

1 Li Chia-mou says: 'To pursue learning is to gain knowledge; to pursue Tao is to get rid of ignorance. The more one knows the more one has to get rid of. Therefore, to increase is but to decrease.'

2 A few lines at the end of this chapter are carried over to Chapter 57.

CHAPTER 49

1 This line is not in Wang Pi's text.

CHAPTER 50

There has been much divergence among different commentators in their interpretations of this chapter, of which Wang Pi's comes most closely to the point. Three parts in ten, says Wang Pi, are roughly taken as one-third or a greater part. The utmost limit of life is three in ten and the utmost limit of death is also three in ten. Men seek too eagerly to live, and their effort takes them beyond the limit of life and still further into the limit of death. The best conserver of life does nothing on purpose to seek to live and therefore he keeps away from the region of death.

1 This line is from Chapter 75.

CHAPTER 51

The last three lines are from Chapter 2.

CHAPTER 52

The very 'beginning' of the Universe is *non-existence*; the 'Mother' is *existence*; the 'children' are *all things*. Cf. Chapter 1.

CHAPTER 53

This chapter has by many been interpreted as Lao Tzu's prophecy about modern civilization. Actually it shows but the evils which have been going on incessantly ever since men deviated from Tao.

1 也 read 施.

CHAPTER 55

1 The man of ample virtue does no harm to anything; therefore nothing harms him.
2 After this, three lines which have already occurred at the end of Chapter 30 are here omitted.

CHAPTER 56

1 Two lines before this are transferred to the beginning of Chapter 81.
2 Two lines after this, which have occurred previously in Chapter 52, are omitted.

CHAPTER 57

1 This and the above line are from Chapter 48.
2 The word 'this' denotes the next eight lines.

CHAPTER 60

1 Wang Pi says: 'When Tao reigns over the world, the spirits are not known as spirits and the Sage is not regarded as sage.'

CHAPTER 62

1 Under this, two lines are shifted to the end of this chapter as a separate paragraph, and one line has been removed to the beginning of Chapter 27.

CHAPTER 63

Notice the order of arrangement of this and the next chapter, which differs greatly from other texts.

CHAPTER 65

Cf. Chapter 48.

CHAPTER 66

1 The first line is from Chapter 32.

CHAPTER 67

1 Cf. the beginning of Chapter 1.
2 From line 9 we can gather that 'not venturing to go ahead of the world' does not mean cowardice.

CHAPTER 69

1 This word comes from the last line of the foregoing chapter.
2 It is the Chinese custom that in an entertainment the host always starts first and the guest follows accordingly; therefore in tactics the host is on the offensive and the guest on the defensive side.

CHAPTER 70

1 In the order of other texts this line comes third.
2 無 read 有.

CHAPTER 73

1 A line reading 'Therefore even the Sage feels a difficulty here' is hereafter omitted according to the Tun-huang text.

CHAPTER 75

1 After this, one sentence which has already occurred in Chapter 50 (lines 6–8) is here omitted.

CHAPTER 76

1 兵 read 折.

CHAPTER 77

1 Cf. Chapter 56.
2 After this one line which has appeared previously in Chapter 51 (lines 10 and 11) is omitted, and another goes to the end of Chapter 81.
3 The last two sentences are from Chapter 81.

CHAPTER 78

1 This line is from Chapter 43.

CHAPTER 79

1 The first line is from Chapter 63.
2 In olden times, the right hand was the honoured side. The Sage keeps to the left, the lower side, in order to be in complete agreement with the holder.

CHAPTER 80

The proposition in this chapter may be regarded as Lao Tzu's idea of Utopia.

CHAPTER 81

1 The first two lines are from Chapter 56.
2 Three lines after this have been transferred to Chapter 77.
3 The last line is from Chapter 77.